Deborah Bardenhagen-

A Visit To The Neighbors

"Mommy, Do You Think Horses Can Talk To Each Other?"

AuthorHouse™
1663 Liberty Drive
Bloomington, IN 47403
www.authorhouse.com
Phone: 1-800-839-8640

© 2012 Deborah Bardenhagen-Ludlow. All Rights Reserved.

No part of this book may be reproduced, stored in a retrieval system,
or transmitted by any means without the written permission of the author.

Published by AuthorHouse 10/25/2012

ISBN: 978-1-4772-8310-3 (sc)
978-1-4772-8311-0 (e)

Library of Congress Control Number: 2012919776

Any people depicted in stock imagery provided by Thinkstock are models,
and such images are being used for illustrative purposes only.
Certain stock imagery © Thinkstock.

This book is printed on acid-free paper.

Because of the dynamic nature of the Internet, any web addresses or links contained in this book may have changed since publication and may no longer be valid. The views expressed in this work are solely those of the author and do not necessarily reflect the views of the publisher, and the publisher hereby disclaims any responsibility for them.

A Visit To The Neighbors

"Mommy, Do You Think Horses Can Talk To Each Other?"

Deborah Bardenhagen-Ludlow

This first book is dedicated to Audrey Mellis who was our neighbor. In her short time with us on earth, she brought the joy of sharing childhood wonder back into my life, as had my children many years prior.

Audrey Mellis
June 19 2009 –
June 9, 2011

Acknowledgements

The idea of publishing a storybook presented itself as I was working on my final project in the completion of my Masters Degree at Spring Arbor University. I love to draw animals and I reflected back on my love of horses since my first encounter, at the age of five, with "Bob's Ponies."

First, I want to thank my mother for her unconditional love throughout my life. My family, Audrey's parents, and the many friends that have offered edits, suggestions, and positive feedback as I worked on this book. I want to thank my children for their love and all they have taught me, their laughter, inspiration, overcoming the obstacles life put before them and for God leading me on this journey.

"Therefore when God has called on his children to write; He gives those words much more power through the Holy Spirit, where he is in control nothing can quench that power" (Regina Burgess, SAU 2012).

Audrey woke up and sat on her bed. She was excited for the day to start. As Audrey looked at her stick horse, she thought about the first time she sat on a horse. It was when she was still a baby.

Audrey thought about the picture her mother took of her on that horse. The horse she sat on was a mother too, with a baby of her own. Audrey could not remember that day, but she wished she could. It was the day she fell in love with horses.

Today Audrey was going to the neighbors' house to feed apples to the horses. When Audrey and her parents got to the barn, the horses were in the pasture eating grass.

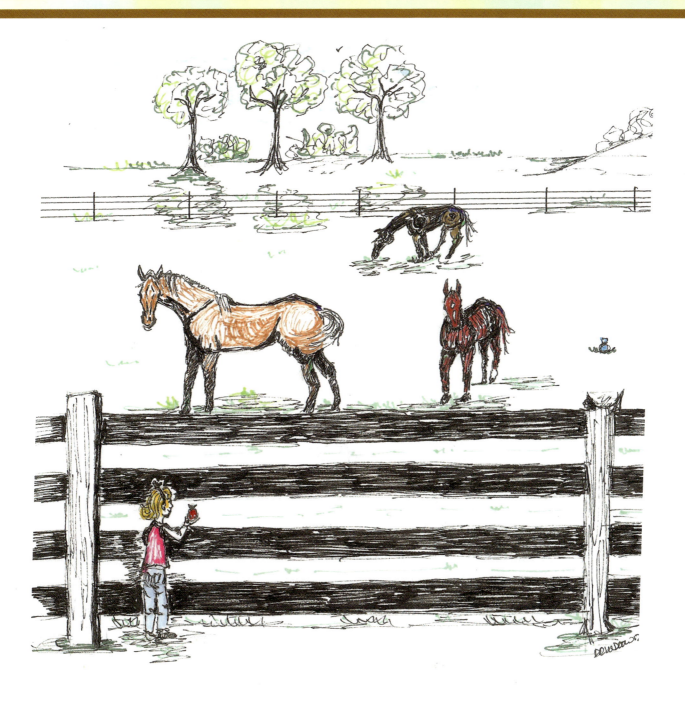

Smarty and Filly looked up, right at Audrey. They were interested in Audrey and her parents. Audrey noticed the horse's ears' pointing forward.

The horses trotted over to see Audrey and her parents. "They are happy and interested to see you Audrey," said Audrey's dad. "How do you know?" asked Audrey. "Because of the way their ears are pointing forward," said Audrey's mom.

Audrey's dad pulled two more apples from his pocket. Suddenly Smarty's ears went back! Smarty looked angry.

"Why did Smarty do that?" asked Audrey. "Smarty wants an apple first, and she's telling the other horses to stay back!" said Audrey's dad.

"How do you know that?" asked Audrey. "Look at her ears. They are laid back, so she looks mad." "If she bites too, then she is really angry," said Audrey's mom.

Suddenly all the horses stopped! Their ears went forward. There was a hot air balloon above the trees. "Look," said Audrey. "The horse's ears are pointing forward. They are interested in that balloon!"

Audrey called out to the horses, "Come over here. I have apples for you." Suddenly, Smarty stopped.   The ball on the ground caught her interest.

The other horses kept moving. Audrey laughed and said, "You better hurry up Smarty. Filly is going to get an apple first."

Audrey and her parents fed the apples to the horses.   When they were done, Audrey said, "Good-bye" and started to walk away, but then Audrey turned around to look at the horses again.

"Look!" said Audrey. "The dog and cat's ears are pointed forward too." "They are interested too," said Audrey's dad. "Because their ears are forward," said Audrey.

The horses were happy and content. They were eating grass again. Audrey turned around to say, good-bye one more time and wondered if the horses were happy. "Do you think they are happy?" she asked her mom.

"Yes they are," said Audrey's mom. You can tell by their ears. They are not forward or back. They are more to the sides and relaxed."Oh, said Audrey. They do look relaxed and happy."

"I love horses!" Audrey said. "Maybe someday I will have a horse of my own and it can live here with these horses."

CPSIA information can be obtained
at www.ICGtesting.com
Printed in the USA
LVIC052030181212
312295LV00003B